Simple Approac

Simple Steps on how to Write a Risk Assessment

Free Offer (Value £50)

Thank you for purchasing this book I hope that what you find from reading through is the confidence to have a go at compiling your own risk assessment where you have experience with the task to be assessed.

I do appreciate that there are going to be times where you will require expert advice such as a regulatory conformance or complex issues but by reading this book, you will gain the confidence and knowledge to compile your own risk assessments for less complex scenarios.

As a thank you from me to you and to give something back if you contact me via email quoting reference **SATS2016-DMB67** you can arrange a free 30 minutes Skype meeting to discuss your topic further and where it fits in with a particular assessment you are working on.

Synopsis

Darren Bedson has a wealth of experience and is a highly qualified health and safety professional who has achieved the standards of being a Chartered Fellow of the 'Institution Occupational Safety and Health'. He has also achieved Fellow Member of the 'International Institute Risk Safety Management; an Incorporated Member of the Association Project Safety', Registered Safety Practitioner with the Occupational Safety Health Consultants Register and, Technician Member of the Institute Fire Engineers.

What you gain from this is expert advice given from a common sense every day approach so you can see health and safety from a different view than being frightened about the consequences if it goes wrong.

Darren has been a safety professional for a great number of years the, last 10 of which he has been Managing Director of BPA Services Limited a Health and Safety Consultancy business which now has over 70 regular clients benefiting from the services on offer.

In addition to the consultancy work, Darren has taken his passion for health and safety to the point of establishing Simple Approach To Safety (SATS) Ltd, availability for keynote speaking and, joining the Professional Speaking Association.

His aim is to speak and get the message across to individuals of all ages that there are big benefits to having a good health and safety approach and, that it is quite simple to achieve.

This book provides a great example to the simplistic approach Darren brings by not weighing you down with regulatory statistics and scaring you but looking at it from an everyday perspective.

If you need to write a risk assessment but, have never done so and, wouldn't know where to start you can be confident that by the time you have read this book you will have a far better understanding and be more than happy to write a risk assessment.

It is appreciated that sometimes the hazard, the risk and the control measures not to mention the legal requirements to comply with regulatory requirements would require a far more robust risk assessment and, in this situation Darren is more than happy to be contacted for further advice where required. The contact details for this are below and at the back of this book.

Telephone: +44 (0) 7427 - 020200

Email: darren@simpleapproachtosafety.com

Website: www.simpleapproachtosafety.com

Acknowledgements

On my journey to where I am so far I have many people to thank for providing me with the courage and confidence to take on the challenges I have overcome and it is only appropriate that I give a big thank you to those people.

It never fails to amaze me just how many people support with their valuable time, advice, assistance and words of encouragement and continue to do so as I follow my life's journey.

There are too many to individually name but they all know who they are and that their support is appreciated.

Chapters

1. Have you written a risk assessment?

2. Writing a risk assessment
    1. Identify the hazard
    2. Decide who might be harmed and how
    3. Evaluate the risks
    4. Record your findings
    5. Review the assessment and revise it if necessary

3. Legal requirements and how you can comply

4. Benefits of a good risk assessment

5. Additional Support

6. Contact Details

Chapter 1

Have you written a Risk Assessment?

Chapter 1

How many risk assessments have you had to carry out in your life?

None?

If we are talking about actually sitting down and writing one from scratch to determine what it is you are doing and how you will achieve it you may be right but let us take a step back and revisit the question.

So, how many risk assessments have you had to carry out in your life?

I would hate to have to guess but if you are at the stage of your life where you are just leaving school at 17 years of age I would say that on average;

- ✓ 1 an hour x 15 hours' x 365 days equals 5475 times a year multiplied by 17 = 93.075 times over your 17 years.

At the age of 30 this would equate to

- ✓ 1 an hour x 15 hours' x 365 days equals 5475 times a year multiplied by 30 = 164,250 times

As a safety professional, I hear on a daily basis people asking me

> "Can you do our risk assessment we've never done one and wouldn't know how to start doing one".

If I asked you now, what do you do?

a) every time you drive your car,
b) every time you cross a road,
c) every time you go out for a walk in adverse weather conditions you would tell me.

When crossing a road, you wouldn't get to the edge of the pavement and step straight off whilst closing your eyes hoping you won't get hit by a bus.

What you would do is firstly look for a pedestrian crossing and if available go to it, press the button then wait until the traffic is stopped by the red light. Even better if there was a footbridge over the road but no crossing available you would use the footbridge.

This way you have removed the hazard, the traffic. As with any risk assessment if you cannot remove the hazard and let's say that there is no foot bridge or pedestrian crossing available then let's look at the thought process.

Hazard

- ✓ Articulated Vehicles,

- ✓ Buses.

- ✓ Cars,

- ✓ Motorcycles,

- ✓ Bicycles.

Risk

- ✓ Getting hit by an artic, bus – potential fatality (you)
- ✓ Getting hit by a car serious life threatening / life changing injury (you)
- ✓ Getting hit by a motorcycle serious life threatening / life changing injury (you and/or motorcyclist)
- ✓ Getting hit by a bicyclist injury (you and/or cyclist)

Control Measures

- ✓ Foot bridge to be used if available
- ✓ Pedestrian crossing to be used if available and foot bridge isn't.
- ✓ Stand back from the edge of the curb.
- ✓ Look left, look right and keep looking until the road is clear.
- ✓ Ensure you keep looking left and right whilst crossing the road.
- ✓ Step on to the pavement and away from the edge of the curb.

Other controls

- ✓ Sensible shoes
- ✓ If dark, bright clothing
- ✓ If a young age have an adult to accompany you.

Risk assessments also ask where we cannot remove the risk part of our controls is to consider what personal protective equipment would we need for our health and safety so, let's now say that in this scenario it is cold, dark, sleeting quite heavily after a substantial snow fall. What personal protective equipment would you use?

The sensible footwear would in most cases be a good pair of wellington boots, there would be a rainproof coat with hood or if no hood on the coat, a hat and probably gloves and scarf to keep you warm and protect your bare neck and hands from the cold.

Collective personal protective equipment is another thing to consider in a risk assessment which then removes any individual error so if you were walking with someone else the chances are you would both be walking under a shared umbrella i.e. collective protective equipment.

Review

The other requirement of a risk assessment is to re-evaluate the situation, check the personal protective equipment for changes in the situation which is a big mistake individual, businesses make as they feel that once a risk assessment is compiled it covers the same task on various projects because in their mind they are doing the same thing every time.

Well, no this definitely is not the case, they are doing the same thing every time but every site is different.

So let's go back to the crossing the road scenario.

You are still crossing the same road which you have done in the same spot every day because it is human nature to do the same thing your mind becomes accustomed to.

Firstly, you may cross the road at the same spot, at the same time, every day but, one day the traffic could be calm because of situations, which have arisen further down the road. You may have a couple of cars and a bicycle to watch out for but, another day you may have an articulated vehicle and the number 25 bus which is today running late to contend with.

This means the hazards are the same to look out for as every other day but, today if you get hit, it goes from an injury to a potential life threatening or fatal incident.

Also on this particular time the weather has taken a dramatic turn for the better, the snow has melted the rain has subsided and there is plenty of spring sunshine with a bit of warmth in the air.

Off comes the wellington boots, hat, scarf, gloves and rainproof coat and instead you have determined that it is warm enough to get away with trainers and a small jacket but, just in case it does rain later you are carrying your umbrella just in case.

> "Health and Safety is common sense
> but
> Common sense isn't that common"

Chapter 2

Writing a risk assessment

Chapter 2

So, now you know what a risk assessment is and how it is structured do you feel as if you could write this down on paper?

To keep it simple for the first one lets continue with the crossing the road scenario because we have already identified the hazards, the risk, the control measures, the required personal protective equipment and, the constant review requirement.

Before continuing with the rest of the book when you turn to the next page to see who is the most experienced person to compile your risk assessment contemplate for a while and have confidence in that person.

Look in to the mirror

Why?

Because you are the individual who performs the task requiring the risk assessment on a day-to-day basis.

Now we have identified how we can use a simple approach to creating a risk assessment we can now take a look at how we can conclude the assessment.

Before we do though we need to understand why, we are doing this, which is controlling the risks in the workplace as part of managing the health and safety of your business.

To do this we need to think about what might cause harm to people and decide whether we are taking reasonable steps to prevent harm. This is known as risk assessment and it is something required by law to carry out.

We also need to remember that a risk assessment is to account for significant risks such as work at height, noise, dust, manual handling, asbestos to name a few and not, to tell us how to boil a kettle, use a microwave or a toaster.

Always retain the common sense simple approach to ensure compliance to your health and safety goals are achieved.

I appreciate that there is a need to prove competence when carrying out health and safety tasks such as managing the workplace, tasks and documents. As I have stated before in this book there will be times where you need to appoint an external professional but, a lot of your day to day basic requirements can be carried out in-house as you are the experts in your business.

So, think about how accidents and ill health could happen and concentrate on real risks, those that are most likely to happen and which will cause the most harm.

For some risks, other regulations require particular control measures. Your assessment can help you identify where you need to look at certain risks and these particular control measures in more detail.

These control measures do not have to be assessed separately but can be considered as part of, or an extension of, your overall risk assessment.

The following pages within this chapter will take a look at the identified areas below.

We are now going to take a look at how we can;
- ✓ Identify the hazard
- ✓ Identify the risk
- ✓ Identify what your control measures are
- ✓ Additional controls
- ✓ Review

Risk assessments in practice – Legal requirements

There are five elements we have to consider whenever we look at completing a risk assessment regardless of the task in hand you can follow this process for every one we do.

The five elements to follow are firstly look for and identify the hazards that are there because of the task you are performing and, or the environment in which the task is being carried out.

Once you have identified the hazards you then have to identify and decide who may be harmed or put at risk as a result of the actions whilst deciding how they would be harmed.

This is not exclusively just the people performing the task but, everyone from other colleagues in the building or, on site, staff associated with other businesses who may share the facilities, visitors and members of the public.

The third action needed is to take is to then evaluate the risks at the same time establishing the control measures you need to take to remove the risk totally or reduce it to an acceptable level.

As an example the first consideration would be do you need to carry out the task such as, let's use the scenario of surveying a gutter or roof ridge for signs of damage.

Instead of getting a ladder and then someone going up to inspect it which creates a dangerous way of work at height with potential serious injuries or fatality you would consider alternative options.

These could be erecting a scaffold by a competent qualified scaffold contractor, scaffold tower by a qualified person or, ideal control would be to use a long handled telescopic camera so you can view from ground level.

Once these first three elements have been completed your next step would be to record your findings so you are then writing it down to be read, understood, discussed and then signed and dated by those performing the task.

This way they are stating that they agree with what you have compiled if they had no initial input in to the compilation of the assessment. An example of a risk assessment bullet point shown below but, remember there is no set format on how you have to write a risk assessment as long as you follow the five step process.

- Task
- Hazard
- Risk
- Who could be harmed
- Likelihood
- Control measures to reduce hazard and risk
- Reduced rating / likelihood

There are several ways that you can identify the likelihood such as a 5x5 scoring matrix, a high, medium and low traffic light system or, Likelihood x Severity.

Severity
1. Trivial Injury
2. Minor Injury
3. Major injury to one person
4. Major injury to several people
5. Fatality

Likelihood

1. Very seldom or never occurs
2. Reasonably likely to occur
3. Certain or, near certain to occur

Severity	5x1	5x2	5x3
	4x1	4x2	4x3
	3x1	3x2	3x3
	2x1	2x2	2x3
	1x1	1x2	1x3
			Likelihood

Finally, once you have got the assessment completed and issued you then need to ensure that you review it regularly to ensure that the hazards and risks are still applicable so that you can revise it as and when required.

Who is responsible for producing the risk assessment?

There are regulatory requirements, which make it a legal requirement to ensure that a competent person produces the risk assessment. Such as 'Management Health and Safety At Work Regulations', 'Lifting Operations Lifting Equipment Regulations', 'Provision Use Work Equipment Regulations' and, 'Construction Design Management

Regulations' whilst it is also a legal requirement for a business owner, director or manager to provide adequate information, instruction, training and supervision.

I would go one step further than this and say that in the years I have been a safety practitioner carrying out accident investigations a lot of the time the causes for these accidents has been down to lack of communication.

With this in mind my thoughts are that it is everyone's responsibility to be involved in production of a risk assessment by communication involving all who are compiling the assessment information.

If you are a machine operator for example and have operated that machine for a long time why wouldn't you be the best placed competent person to be involved in producing the assessment of it.

Yes, I do admit that there will be a need sometimes for a specialist safety person to ensure that what you are writing is in compliance with the regulation specific to your industry or machine but, they will not be as competent as you when it comes to knowing the hazards and risks you face daily.

There will also be times when you cannot compile a risk assessment such as when it involves chemicals or dangerous processes in which case you will require the services of a DSEAR specialist (Dangerous Substances Explosives Atmosphere Regulations).

Health and Safety At Work Etc. Act 1974

The health and safety at work etc. act was implemented in 1974 and to this day is the main act that drives health and safety in the workplace by ensuring everyone is provided with the correct information, instruction, training and supervision to allow them to leave home to go to work and return at the end of their working day.

There are several sections within this Act but for the purpose of this book I am going to mention just a couple although you can access the full Act on the Health and Safety Executive (HSE) website at www.HSE.org.uk

What the Act does state is that employers will, as far as is reasonably practicable ensure the health, safety and welfare at work of all employees and, provide such information, instruction, training and supervision as is necessary to do so.

Before I move on I would like to highlight a particular misconception that I seem to come across quite regularly which is that when I am talking to business owners or Directors they do not account for everyone they should be including when they follow the requirements.

This seems to be more so in the construction industry when I get told that as an example 'oh, we have four employees so we don't need to do this'.

Sorry to be the bearer of bad news but even if it was one person you do need to do a risk assessment and, once I ask them 'does this include the directors?' they say no me and my wife own the business.

This maybe the case but you are still employees of the company and then I find out they employ lots of sub-contractors on a regular basis.

What I am getting at is that when you fulfil the requirements for compliance the welfare, information, instruction etc. also has to be considered for all these people also.

What do I have to do as an employee?

As we have briefly determined there are many requirements set on an employer which go in to great detail in the Act but, as employees we have a duty also to take care of our own health and safety and that of others who may be affected by our acts and omissions.

Basically this statement in the Act means that before we perform a task we should be considering firstly do we need to do it then, follow the remaining four steps of the risk assessment process whilst taking into account those who could be harmed as well as ourselves.

We also have to co-operate with our employer at all times in relation to health and safety and use appropriate equipment which they have supplied use in accordance with training and instruction.

Where we fail to follow reasonable instruction for our health and safety or. Use the equipment incorrectly following training our employer is within their rights to discipline us and take appropriate action.

A guide to risk assessment requirements

There are many regulations that require risks to be assessed and certain risks are covered by more than one or these regulations as an example if you have already assessed the risks and the precautions that must be taken to comply with one regulation you do not need to repeat it all again.

Some of the common risk provisions are required within the regulations given below although this list is not exhaustive so please be aware that there are a lot more which is where it may be deemed necessary to appoint a specialist consultant.

- Management of Health and Safety at Work Regulations 1999
- Manual Handling Operations Regulations 1992 (as amended 2002 – Manual Handling Regulations)

- Personal Protective Equipment at Work Regulations 1992
- Health and Safety (Display Screen Equipment) Regulations 1992 (as amended 2002 – Display Screen Regulations)
- Noise at Work Regulations 2005
- Control of Asbestos Regulations 2006

So, lets summarise what we have just gone through in this section regarding legal requirements for risk assessments.

Procedure when completing a risk assessment is;

- Look for and identify the hazards
- Decide who might be harmed and how
- Evaluate the risks and implement control measures to eliminate or reduce the risk
- Record the findings of the assessment, and
- Review, revise the assessment.

Who has to assess the risks?

In all cases employers and self-employed people are responsible for assessing the risk and seeing that it is adequately carried out because they know first-hand what the risks in their workplace are and, will often be able to offer practicable solutions to controlling the risk.

Even if you have deemed it necessary to appoint a specialist consultant, as an example DSEAR you would still be required to have an involvement in the production of the assessment.

The management regulations require the employer to assess the risks to the health and safety of anyone that may be affected by your activities, you, fellow workers, other people employees where there is a conflict and, members of the public.

The exception to this requirement is manual handling which is yourself and fellow workers involved in the handling process for that particular task.

What risks should be assessed?

As an employer or employee you are required to examine what in your workplace could cause harm to people so that you can determine whether you have taken enough precautions or, should do more to meet what the law says you must do.

The risk assessment provisions in all regulations say that your assessment of risks must either be 'adequate' or 'suitable' and sufficient.

This means that you do not have to over-complicate the assessment. You must judge if the hazards are significant and if you have them covered by satisfactory precautions so that the risks are eliminated or reduced.

Before you carry out any task that has significant risks associated with it you have to assess the risks in your workplace before you begin any new tasks or, review the assessment if there is already one in place.

Many of the specific regulations e.g. COSHH (Control of Substances Hazardous to Health) tell you that you cannot start work before you have assessed the risks they cover.

Recording the assessment

If you have a company which employs five or more people including the directors and sub-contracted regular workers, then you must record the significant findings in your written assessment.

However, if you have to do specific things that the risk assessment of the Noise at Work Regulations or, the Control of Asbestos Regulations require then, you have to keep records of every assessment even if there are less than five employees.

Once you have compiled the assessment and it has been read, understood and discussed with all people involved then you have to ensure that it is readily available for the people carrying out the task to be able to retrieve it for review or, for auditing purposes.

All regulations require a review of the assessment and revision as necessary and as a minimum every twelve months where the task has not changed.

This has to be sooner if you suspect that the assessment is no longer valid or there has been significant change either to the task or, the work area.

How we can reduce this risk

So, the five steps to the risk assessment requires us to first of all identify the hazard and the risk.

To enable us to do this we need to know what the difference is between a hazard and a risk.

Hazard, means anything that has the potential to cause harm such as chemicals, electricity, working from ladders as an example.

Risk is the chance high or low that somebody will be harmed by the hazard such as someone using a ladder the hazard, who falls off and breaks their leg from the landing, the risk is fall from height.

1 - Identify the hazard

By doing a walk around your workplace you can look around to look at what could reasonably be expected to cause harm whilst ignoring the trivial issues.

Concentrate on the significant hazards which could result in serious harm or affect several people and ask others what they as they may notice things that you don't.

Another requirement is to reference manufacturers' instructions or data sheets, accident and ill-health records as they can also help you spot hazards and put risks in their true perspective.

Identifying a trend of accidents, incidents and near-misses which have been recorded is a great way of identifying hazards so enlist the support from your human resource department or consultant when doing this.

2 – Identify the risk

When identifying the risk decide who may be harmed don't forget specific people such as young workers, trainees, new and expectant mothers all, of who may be put at particular risk from the activity.

A group of people that genuinely get missed out of consideration are visitors, contractors, maintenance workers and, cleaners who may not be in the workplace at the time.

When I go out to businesses to carry out an assessment where applicable I will review their COSHH assessments but these nearly always only cover the person actually carrying out the activity.

The person compiling the assessment or, the Director responsible always seem to forget about the cleaner who may come in to premises at 6am to clean up and use chemicals for cleaning but, never compile an assessment for them or even train the cleaner.

I do appreciate that you would say 'well their company should do that' and, yes you are correct but these are generic for the chemical being used and do not take in to account the working environment, anything that could potentially react to the chemical they are using.

Also the fact that whilst they are on your premises it is your responsibility to ensure that they have been given the correct information, instruction and training.

Finally, also consider members of the public or people who share your workplace if there is any chance that they could be hurt by your activities.

3 – Evaluate the risks

When evaluating the risk consider how likely it is that each hazard could cause harm as this will determine if you need to do more to reduce the risk.

Even after all precautions have been taken some risks usually remain so you have to decide for each significant hazard if the remaining risk is high, medium or low.

What cannot be accepted is that you start with a rating of high and then finish with a rating of high after your control measures are in place it must always reduce the risk i.e. high too medium/low or, medium too low.

If the control measure does not achieve this, you need to put more control measures in or re-assess the ones you have put in to place already.

First, ask yourself have you done all the things that the law says you have got to do, e.g. access to dangerous parts of a machine have stringent regulations to ensure that guards are fitted.

If you find that something needs to be done, draw up an action list and give priority to any remaining risks which are high and, or those which could affect most people.

Ask yourself, can I get rid of the hazard altogether?

If not how can I control the risks so that harm is unlikely?

By applying the principles below in the correct order of priority you can control the risk where you have not managed to eliminate it altogether.

a) Try a less risky option
b) Prevent access to the hazard e.g. guarding, barriers.
c) Organise the work to reduce exposure to the hazard
d) Issue personal protective equipment
e) Provide welfare facilities such as washing for the removal of contamination before consuming food or drink.

Please remember though that these principles are assuming that you have already employed competent people to perform the task via providing them with the required training or licenses to do so.

4 – Record your findings

When you write a risk assessment there is no set way required to do so as long as it is legible but, they must, be suitable and sufficient so you do need to be able to show that you have completed the following.

First that you carried out a proper check and you involved those who may be affected by asking them questions, getting them to walk around with you and assessing existing assessments.

Did you deal with all the obvious significant hazards taking into account the number of people who could be involved and, the precautions are reasonable to result in the remaining risks are low.

Once you have achieved this keep a written record for future reference or use as it can help you if an inspector asks what precautions you have taken or, if you become involved in any action for liability such as an accident claim against you.

It will also prove that you have done what the law requires you to do but, more importantly than all this it proves that you have a genuine interest in the safety of others and good morals as a business.

5 – Review the assessment and revise it if necessary

When you bring in new machines, substances and procedures which could lead to new hazards review the assessment but, do not amend for every trivial change.

If you introduce a new job which creates significant new hazards, then you will need to consider them and do whatever you need to keep the risks down.

When doing this follow the same process as you did initially and involve others as well as reviewing existing documents.

The key thing to remember is that it is good practice to review all risk assessments from time to time to make sure that the precautions are still working effectively.

'Best practice is doing the minimum required **not**, just achieving what you need to do'

Chapter 3

Legal requirements and how you can comply

Chapter 3

As we have determined people think that the legal requirement for recording a risk assessment in writing is exempt if fewer than five employees are employed within the business and as long as you can prove a risk assessment has been carried out then maybe but, how do you prove this.

One piece of advice I will give on this though is if you choose not to do an assessment in writing is that you need to include Directors of the business when working out if you have fewer than five because Directors are employees of the business.

Legally you should carry out a risk assessment before you do any work which presents a risk of injury or ill health to you as the person carrying out the task or those likely to be affected by the outcome if you are an employer or a self-employed person.

As an employer or self-employed person you legally have to carry out a risk assessment of the health and safety risks arising out of the work.

The outcome of carrying out the risk assessment is to identify what needs to be done to control health and safety risks.

As an employer or a self-employed person you are responsible for health and safety in your business for employees, sub-contracted persons, and those affected by your activities and although you can delegate the task, you are ultimately responsible so please make sure that whoever does the risk assessment is competent to do so.

A competent person should involve those who carry out the task in the process so conversations can be carried out between the person undertaking the assessment and those who perform the task which helps to identify risks from both mind-sets.

As we have ascertained you do not necessarily need specific training or qualifications to carry out a risk assessment, however, you must appoint someone competent to help you meet your health and safety duties.

A competent person is someone with the necessary skills, knowledge and experience to manage health and safety and the appointment can be one or a combination of yourself, one or more of your workers or, someone from outside your business.

Once you have identified who will be part of the team creating the risk assessment and it has been implemented to those performing the task you then legally should review your risk assessment if it is no longer valid or, if there has been a significant change to the process or individuals involved.

Your workplace will change over time for a number of possible reasons such as bringing in new equipment, substances and procedures.

There may be advances in technology that you wish to keep up to date with to aid production or it may be that you have experienced an accident incident or near miss in the workplace.

If any of these events happen, you should review and update your risk assessment then ensure that it is implemented by making it available to those who are likely to be affected.

There is no set frequency for carrying out a review of an assessment although I would advise that it is good working practice to do so at least on an annual basis.

I say this for a number of reasons from refreshing your memory on what your controls where if nothing has changed, identifying shortfalls which may have arisen such as people not following the control methods to, noting that something is not working as it should so needs to be changed.

Remember though that when producing a risk assessment, it is not about creating large volumes of paperwork but about identifying sensible measures to control the risks in your workplace.

You are probably already taking steps to protect your employees, but your risk assessment will help you decide whether you have covered all you need to.

There are also some regulations which require a risk assessment for your workplace regardless of how many people are involved for example a fire risk assessment.

A fire risk assessment is a legal requirement under the 'Regulatory Reform (Fire Safety) Order 2005 but the person responsible for ensuring this happens will depend on your tenancy agreement as to whether it is your landlord or yourself.

Once in place the fire risk assessment has to be reviewed every two years or sooner if there are significant changes to the layout or processes.

Another example of when an assessment has to be carried out regardless of number of people affected is the need for an asbestos management survey assessment on any workplace building which was built prior to the year 2000.

This is to be reviewed annually where asbestos containing materials are identified but left in because they are in good condition.

The exception to this rule is if you are having any refurbishment or major works carried out on the property in which case you would require an Asbestos Refurbishment / Demolition Report before authorisation can be given for any work to commence on disturbance of the fabric of the building.

This is because the management survey is structured for ongoing management of the building and minor maintenance works such as gas or electrical services that are not disturbing the fabric.

"Having Health and Safety is Expensive"

"Try,

not having health and safety then see how expensive it can be"

Free Offer (Value £50)

Don't forget that as a thank you for purchasing this book I am willing to give something back if you contact me via email quoting reference **SATS2016-DMB67**.

Upon contacting me quoting this reference number we can arrange a time and date for your free 30 minutes Skype meeting to discuss your topic further and where it fits in with a particular assessment you are working on.

Chapter 4
Benefits of a good risk assessment

Chapter 4

The overall main benefit of a good risk assessment is that everyone involved in the tasks which the assessment covers are made aware of the hazards, risks and control measures that means they go home safely at the end of the working day.

This is not the only benefit though although the main one as there are several other benefits from enforcing a proactive approach to health and safety via the production of sufficiently developed risk assessments.

Some businesses look at the cost outlay incurred in employing someone in-house or external as an advisor and decide against doing so hoping nothing happens.

This is fine as long as nothing happens but, they need to realise there are potentially massive costs when it doesn't.

The major cost may be an injury to an individual which whether minor or life changing has a negative impact on moral within the business as well as the costs you will face from fines, court costs, and poor publicity, lost time cover and so on.

When your organisation demonstrates that you have considered all tasks the employees are required to carry out which have significant risks you will find that employees are reciprocating this approach by making you aware of issues, risks or concerns so they become your eyes and ears.

They are more willing to carry out any statutory machinery inspections, fire safety inspections and, general workplace inspections as they know that the paperwork will not just gather dust on a manager's desk but, be actioned as soon as possible.

Having risk assessments in place not only provides a feel good factor within your organisation they also show clients and potential clients that you take health and safety seriously and have thought through the task that you will be undertaking on behalf of them.

I have seen organisations lose out on major projects which would have generated a good return on investment if they had suitable risk assessments in place so the money which could be generated in new business is potentially very lucrative.

Imagine tendering for a new project which is worth £100,000 to your business and then being rejected for consideration because you cannot demonstrate in the pre-qualification questionnaire or tender pack that you have a robust risk assessment in place to demonstrate how the work will be carried out safely, how would you feel?

Gutted?

If you employ an in-house health and safety person to do your risk assessments the initial outlay of cost would probably be £30 or, utilising an external consultant on average would be potentially anything between £100 to £150.

I appreciate it sounds a lot of money to outlay if you are not guaranteed the work but the possibility of getting a return on investment of £99.850.00 is one worth taking because on average you can afford to miss out on a few tenders as long as you win the occasional one.

So, let's look at some other benefits of having a good, robust risk assessment in place.

Absence of workers from work costs is a considerable amount of money so by improving health and safety measures at the workplace reduces the likelihood that people will need to take sick leave and save money on the direct costs of absence.

If you lose an employee from work you are going to be paying the salary of the absent employee whilst they are absent which could be one day upwards depending on the reason for this.

You may say that your policy does not include payment for absenteeism from work which is fine but, if it is a genuine case which has been a result of an incident at work you are likely to face a claim for loss of earnings at the very least.

Other costs incurred will be for payment of overtime other employees covering for the absent employee and loss of output incurred by the absent employee.

If your absent employee is age 25 or over and on the national minimum wage you would be paying them £7.20 per hour.

For the purpose of this example let's assume that they have had an accident at work which has resulted in one-week absence from work which is 36 hour working week.

So firstly you are paying out £259.20 to the absent employee then that the person's absence is being covered by an agency worker. Once the agency worker who is also on minimum pay and, the agency mark-up has been paid it may cost you £10 per hour equating to £360.

Your absent employee may be experienced in the role they carry out so are very productive but the agency worker will need to be inducted and supervised until a point that they are competent enough to be left not needing a one to one supervision all of which costs money.

As you can see from this example as a very minimum your absent employee has cost an additional £360. What would this mean if they were off work for let's say, five weeks so straight away this is a cost of £1800.

If, thereafter as a result of the absence a claim is issued against you for failure to provide a risk assessment, suitable information, training or supervision then this could escalate tenfold.

By having the risk assessments in place suitably developed and everyone is aware of the existence of the assessment you can then save money on the indirect costs of absence.

You will not need to spend on the time it will take for a replacement to learn the new role and become productive and loss of business, continuity and reputation but can put that money saved to ongoing development of your employees through additional training and incentives.

The sooner you take positive action to reduce absence, the sooner your sick employee can return to work successfully and get on with helping you build your business.

When an agency worker is required there are costs to outlay for training replacement staff and possible drops in productivity as a new staff member comes up to speed with the work required on the post so again keeping your employees at work all have cost effective benefits as well as good moral.

By maintaining a good standard of health and safety in the workplace you could lower insurance premiums giving you more money in the bank.

Most insurance companies will now carry out an health and safety audit on your business before committing to insuring you so by having assessments in place this will support your lower premiums.

You are responsible for the health and safety of your employees while they are at work. With very few exceptions, employers must have Employer Liability

Compulsory Insurance to cover for injuries and ill health experienced by their employees while at work.

Insurance costs do not necessarily cover sick pay, lost time, overtime working and temporary labour so you will need to make sure you know what the cover is.

Some insurance premiums can cover insurance investigation time, fines and, legal costs but this would be again identified at the time of taking out the insurance cover.

Uninsured costs can outweigh the insured costs - and these uninsured costs come straight off your company's 'bottom-line' profits. Poor health and safety procedures could mean increased insurance premiums or difficulty in obtaining future insurance cover.

A key benefit of having a good health and safety standard is that you keep your reputation because preventing accidents and ill health at work helps you build a good reputation with your clients, your workers and associates.

It takes years to build a positive and respectable image for your business but seconds to destroy it so it is vital that your business keeps that good name. Good public relations increase sales and generate more leads.

If your company comes into disrepute for any reason, including avoidable injury or accidents in the work environment, or continued employee ill health, it can cost you more than replacing that member of staff.

You can expect negative public opinion that is hard to reverse, fines, unwanted attention from pressure groups, disastrous sales, reduced profits and revenue. This could take time to recover and get your business up and running again.

It is easy to prevent damage to your health and safety reputation by implementing a simple and effective programme of control to manage the risks and improve productivity,

Improving health and safety helps you improve morale and productivity in your business. Your workers can do their work with less difficulty and less danger.

They will appreciate improvements you make to their working environment. This can save you money and add to your profitability in the long run.

Stress and accidents at work are two of the biggest causes of absence from work today. Whether they cause short, unscheduled absences or long-term illness, they can have a serious impact on your productivity and profits.

If workers have to cover for an absent colleague it can put additional pressures on them, contributing to increased absence in the longer term.

Chapter 5
Additional Support

Chapter 5

I come across lots of businesses who employ full time health and safety people who have worked their way up through the organisation and have a vast wealth of knowledge on the business tasks.

These are really good to have as they recognise the tasks requirements when discussing with the person who will be performing the task so they can associate what is to be done with the risks that are there to control.

Where businesses do this they also appreciate a comfort buffer to ensure that the person doing that role is supported and advised where required as they may know everything about the organisation but, fall short where it comes to legislative requirements and ever changing compliance requirements.

Current regulation is to be complied with so this is where an external consultant is a valuable addition to the team which gives you the benefit of having an in-house person who is familiar with your business activities whilst the external competent advisor will be beneficial from a regulatory compliant view.

My advice when appointing an external consultant is not to look at cost only as the driving force in your decision making but, ask yourself can you work with this person, are they understanding your requirements, do they come with references or recommendation from businesses in your sector.

All these regulations can be found on the internet with the Health and Safety Executive website a great place to find a lot of this information. www.hse.gov.uk

There are also some other fantastic sources of information on the internet some of which are.

www.iosh.co.uk

www.iirsm.org

www.aps.org.uk

www.citb,co.uk

Chapter 6

Contact Details

Chapter 6

As I mentioned earlier a lot of the time the compilation of risk assessments can be compiled in-house by someone who has experience in the task we are assessing.

Despite this there is also a need to be aware of the specific requirements for assessment identified in a current regulation which is all available on the internet if you look as demonstrated in the last chapter.

Where you feel that there is a need for additional support on compiling risk assessments, safe operating procedures, policies, procedures or general consultancy services either as a one-off, ad-hoc or retained basis I can be contacted via the details later in this book.

My keynote speaking sessions are available for all organisations with the topic and length of talk structured to your need.

Although topics are bespoke to each booking there is a general structure which is a simple approach to safety i.e. get the message across to you and your delegates in a manner that doesn't baffle them with complex information.

This message is important to me hence having long-term retained clients who renew year on year.

Far too many people over complicate the way they carry out their health and safety duties which is either through lack of understanding or for self-indulgence and importance.

There are two main topics which we provide, they are;

1. Risk Assessments – Simple Steps and,

2. What is the real cost of not having health and safety?

There are opportunities to book Darren for keynote speaking on other subject matters so do not hesitate to contact us if you do, wish to discuss your requirements.

If you wish to find out how you can book a session contact Darren at the details given and request a booking brochure which will explain more about the my fees.

Contact Details;

Darren Bedson

CFIOSH – FIIRSM – IMaPS – OSHCR – TIFireE - MPSA

Chartered Fellow and Registered Safety Practitioner

Member Professional Speakers Association

+44 (0) 7427 020200

darren@simpleapproachtosafety.com

www.simpleapproachtosafety.com

Thank you for purchasing and reading through this book I hope that it has delivered what was expected and you can now go away with having the confidence to give it a go and write your own risk assessment.

Please take advantage of the opportunity to receive a free 30 minute Skype meeting either before you have a go at writing a risk assessment to confirm your required actions or, after you have written the assessment so we can discuss what you have completed and provide feedback during the meeting.

Printed in Great Britain
by Amazon